Making
Mistake

Di Taylor

Name _____

Age _____

Class _____

OXFORD
UNIVERSITY PRESS

OXFORD
UNIVERSITY PRESS

Great Clarendon Street, Oxford OX2 6DP

Oxford University Press is a department of the University of Oxford.
It furthers the University's objective of excellence in research, scholarship,
and education by publishing worldwide in

Oxford New York

Auckland Cape Town Dar es Salaam Hong Kong Karachi
Kuala Lumpur Madrid Melbourne Mexico City Nairobi
New Delhi Shanghai Taipei Toronto

With offices in

Argentina Austria Brazil Chile Czech Republic France Greece
Guatemala Hungary Italy Japan Poland Portugal Singapore
South Korea Switzerland Thailand Turkey Ukraine Vietnam

OXFORD and OXFORD ENGLISH are registered trade marks of
Oxford University Press in the UK and in certain other countries

ISBN: 978 0 19 440097 8

Printed in China

ACKNOWLEDGEMENTS

Illustrations by: Andy Hamilton

With thanks to Sally Spray for her contribution to this series

Reading Dolphins
Notes for teachers & parents

📖 Using the book

1 Begin by looking at the first story page (page 2). Look at the picture and ask questions about it. Then read the story text under the picture with your students. **Use section 1 of the CD for this if possible.**

2 Teach and check the understanding of any new vocabulary. Note that some of the words are in the **Picture Dictionary** at the back of the book.

3 Now look at the activities on the right-hand page. Show the example to the students and instruct them to complete the activities. This may be done individually, in pairs, or as a class.

4 Do the same for the remaining pages of the book.

5 Retell the whole story more quickly, reinforcing the new vocabulary. **Sections 2 and 3 of the CD can help with this.**

6 **If possible, listen to the expanded story (section 4 of the CD). The students should follow in their books.**

7 When the book is finished, use the **Picture Dictionary** to check that students understand and remember new vocabulary. **Section 5 of the CD can help with this.**

💿 Using the CD

The CD contains five sections.

1 The story told slowly, with pauses. Use this during the first reading. It may also be used for "Listen and repeat" activities at any point.

2 The story told at normal speed. This should be used once the students have read the book for the first time.

3 The story chanted. Students may want to chant along with the story.

4 The expanded story. The story is told in a longer version. This will help the students understand English when it is spoken faster, as they will now know the story and the vocabulary.

5 Vocabulary. Each word in the **Picture Dictionary** is spoken and then used in a simple sentence.

Cindy, I'm busy. Can you go to the supermarket for me?

Sure Mom. Matt can help me.

Circle yes or no .

❶ Cindy is at home.　　　yes / no

❷ Matt is in the supermarket.　　yes / no

❸ Cindy's mother is busy.　　yes / no

❹ Cindy has a sister.　　yes / no

❺ Matt has a brother.　　yes / no

❻ It is three o'clock.　　yes / no

❼ Cindy wants to help.　　yes / no

❽ Cindy is Matt's sister.　　yes / no

We need some apples, rice, grapes, cream, butter, corn, potatoes, and some cheese.

1 Look at page 4. Find and circle.

r	i	c	e	I	c	l
i	k	r	a	e	o	b
s	h	e	p	o	r	u
g	r	a	p	e	n	t
p	p	m	l	i	n	t
g	c	h	e	e	s	e
p	o	t	a	t	o	r

2 Look at the uncircled letters.
Find and write the secret sentence.

I _ _ _ _ _ _ _ _ _ _ _ _ _ .

Oh no! I forgot the shopping
list at home.

That's OK! I can remember
what we need.

What do they need? Write.

Shopping List

apples
_____

_____

_____

_____

_____

_____

_____

Did Mommy say we need some apples?

No, not apples. She said apple pie.

Write in alphabetical order.

 banana    apple   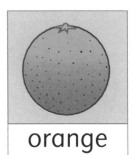 orange

 apple       strawberry

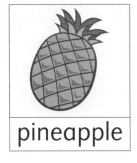 pineapple       lemon

 grapes       watermelon

9

We need some rice.

No, not rice. I think Mommy wants rice pops!

I like rice pops for breakfast.

Rearrange the words.

❶ Cindy's   is   Matt   brother.

Matt is Cindy's brother.

❷ shopping   Matt   and   are   Cindy.

_____

❸ home   is   Cindy's   at   mother.

_____

❹ shopping   Cindy   forgot   list   the.

_____

❺ his   is   sister   helping   Matt.

_____

❻ pops   rice   Cindy   eat   to   likes.

_____

Mommy wants some cream.

No, not cream. We need ice cream. Chocolate ice cream is my favorite.

Write There is or There are.

❶ <u>There</u> <u>are</u> some oranges.

❷ _____ _____ some apples.

❸ _____ _____ an apple pie.

❹ _____ _____ some ice cream.

❺ _____ _____ some rice.

❻ _____ _____ a box of
rice pops.

❼ _____ _____ two children.

❽ _____ _____ many things.

Mommy wants some potatoes for dinner.

Let's get some potato chips. Daddy likes potato chips.

Write.

Mom needs some apples, but
Matt wants some apple pie.

Mommy wants grapes.

I am thirsty. I want some grape soda.

Good idea! I am thirsty, too.

Answer the questions.

❶ Are Cindy and Matt shopping?

Yes, they are.

❷ Do you like to go shopping?

_____

❸ Do they have a shopping list?

_____

❹ Can they remember what their mother needs?

_____

❺ Does Cindy like grape soda?

_____

❻ Does Mommy want grapes?

_____

Did Mommy say we need corn?

Mommy likes popcorn.

OK. Let's get some popcorn.

Match and write.

base super
paper sun
bed pop
water ice flower
market melon
corn room
ball
cream news

baseball _____

_____ _____

_____ _____

_____ _____

Mommy wants some butter and cheese.

I think she wants peanut butter and cheeseburgers.

Write the correct letter.

❶ Cindy is a
A mother
B boy
C girl
.

C

❷ Matt is
A his
B its
C her
brother.

❸ Mommy
A has
B needs
C likes
rice.

❹ They are
A in
B to
C by
the supermarket.

❺ They
A are
B is
C am
shopping.

❻ Matt
A are
B is
C am
helping.

21

Do we have everything on the shopping list?

I think so.

Write the story.

Cindy and Matt are brother ___and___ sister. Their mother is _____, so they help her to do the _____. They go to the _____. They don't buy apples. They buy _____. They don't buy rice. They buy _____. They don't buy cream. They buy _____. They don't buy potatoes. They buy _____. They don't buy grapes. They buy _____. They don't buy corn. They buy _____. They don't buy butter. They buy _____. They don't buy cheese. They buy _____.

Cindy and Matt are _____.

Picture Dictionary

apple pie    cheeseburger

banana   corn

butter   cream

cart    grapes

cheese   ice cream

lemon

potato chips

orange

rice

peanut butter

rice pops

pineapple

soda

popcorn

strawberry

potato

watermelon

Dolphin Readers

Dolphin Readers are available at five levels, from Starter to 4.

The Dolphins series covers four major themes:

Grammar, Living Together, The World Around Us, Science and Nature.

For each theme, there are two titles at every level.

Activity Books are available for all Dolphins.

All Dolphins are available on audio CD.
(2 TITLES ON EACH CD SEE TABLE BELOW)

Teacher's Notes are available at **www.oup.com/elt/dolphins**

	Grammar	Living Together	The World Around Us	Science and Nature
Starter	• Silly Squirrel • Monkeying Around	• My Family • A Day with Baby	• Doctor, Doctor • Moving House	• A Game of Shapes • Baby Animals
Level 1	• Meet Molly • Where Is It?	• Little Helpers • Jack the Hero	• On Safari • Lost Kitten	• Number Magic • How's the Weather?
Level 2	• Double Trouble • Super Sam	• Candy for Breakfast • Lost!	• A Visit to the City • Matt's Mistake	• Numbers, Numbers Everywhere • Circles and Squares
Level 3	• Students in Space • What Did You Do Yesterday?	• New Girl in School • Uncle Jerry's Great Idea	• Just Like Mine • Wonderful Wild Animals	• Things That Fly • Let's Go to the Rainforest
Level 4	• The Tough Task • Yesterday, Today and Tomorrow	• We Won the Cup • Up and Down	• Where People Live • City Girl, Country Boy	• In the Ocean • Go, Gorillas, Go